Ezekiel

'The message of Ezekiel has profound importance for today. In these simple but profound devotional thoughts, Liam Goligher cuts to the heart in two ways. First, he gets to the heart of the truth that we find in Ezekiel. Second, he cuts to the heart of the human longing for God. These words inspire, challenge and comfort in equal measure. They remind us that God is closer than we think and that hope is deeper than we could imagine.'
The Revd Malcolm Duncan, Lead Pastor, Gold Hill Baptist Church

'In the face of both national and personal crisis, Ezekiel is called by God as a prophet, not in Jerusalem, but in Babylon. Liam Goligher provides us with refreshing and challenging insights on the prophet's words and relevance for us in the UK in the twenty-first century.'
Steve Clifford, Director, Evangelical Alliance UK

30-DAY DEVOTIONAL

Ezekiel

Liam Goligher
with Elizabeth McQuoid

Keswick
Resources

FOOD
FOR THE
JOURNEY

INTER-VARSITY PRESS
36 Causton Street, London SW1P 4ST, England
Email: ivp@ivpbooks.com
Website: www.ivpbooks.com

First published 2017

British Library Cataloguing-in-Publication Data
A catalogue record for this book is available from the British Library.

ISBN: 978–1–78359–603–4
eBook ISBN: 978–1–78359–604–1

Typeset in Great Britain by CRB Associates, Potterhanworth, Lincolnshire
Printed in Great Britain by Ashford Colour Press Ltd, Gosport, Hampshire

Inter-Varsity Press publishes Christian books that are true to the Bible and that communicate
the gospel, develop discipleship and strengthen the church for its mission in the world.

IVP originated within the Inter-Varsity Fellowship, now the Universities and Colleges
Christian Fellowship, a student movement connecting Christian Unions in universities and
colleges throughout Great Britain, and a member movement of the International Fellowship
of Evangelical Students. Website: www.uccf.org.uk. That historic association is maintained,
and all senior IVP staff and committee members subscribe to the UCCF Basis of Faith.

Preface

Can you guess how many sermons have been preached from the Keswick platform? Almost 6,500!

For over 140 years, the Keswick Convention in the English Lake District has welcomed gifted expositors from all over the world. The convention's archive is a treasure trove of sermons preached on every book of the Bible.

This series is an invitation to mine that treasure. It takes talks from the Bible Reading series given by well-loved Keswick speakers, past and present, and reformats them into daily devotionals. Where necessary, the language has been updated but, on the whole, it is the message you would have heard had you been listening in the tent on Skiddaw Street. Each day of the devotional ends with a newly written section designed to help you apply God's Word to your own life and situation.

Whether you are a convention regular or have never been to Keswick, this Food for the Journey series is a unique opportunity to study the Scriptures with a Bible teacher by your side. Each book is designed to fit in your jacket pocket or handbag so you can read it anywhere – over the breakfast table, on the commute into work or college, while you are waiting in your car, during your lunch break or in bed at night. Wherever life's journey takes you, time in God's Word is vital nourishment for your spiritual journey.

Our prayer is that these devotionals become your daily feast, a precious opportunity to meet with God through his Word. Read, meditate, apply and pray through the Scriptures given for each day, and allow God's truths to take root and transform your life.

If these devotionals whet your appetite for more, there is a 'For further study' section at the end of each book. You can also visit our website at <www.keswickministries.org/resources> to find the full range of books, study guides, CDs, DVDs and mp3s available. Why not order an audio recording of the Bible Reading series to accompany your daily devotional?

Let the word of Christ dwell in you richly.
(Colossians 3:16, ESV)

Introduction
Ezekiel

What has been your most memorable birthday?

Ezekiel ben Buzi would certainly never forget his thirtieth birthday.

He had been trained as a priest and brought up to believe that when he turned thirty his life's work would begin. He had spent years anticipating this moment when he would be ordained and eligible to serve in the temple. So you would forgive Ezekiel if he woke up feeling discouraged on his birthday.

Instead of being in Jerusalem he was a captive in Babylon. In 605 King Nebuchadnezzar had subdued Judah and taken some hostages back to Babylon, including Daniel and his three friends. A few years later Judah's King Jehoiakim rebelled. Nebuchadnezzar conquered Jerusalem and along with the temple treasure took some of the nobles, royal family and priests back with him to Babylon. Among the group was this trainee priest. The day that Ezekiel turned thirty he was five years into his captivity in Babylon.

To say that life hadn't turned out as Ezekiel had anticipated is probably an understatement. Instead of being a priest, he was called by God to be a prophet. Instead of living in the holy city of Jerusalem, he was an exile in Babylon. Instead of serving in the temple, he was surrounded by a plethora of pagan gods.

But on his thirtieth birthday God gave Ezekiel a vision.

Many of the exiles were having a crisis of faith. These displaced Jews were wondering where God was. Had he been defeated by the Babylonian gods? If he was still in control, why didn't he intervene? Ezekiel's timely vision confronted the Jews with their sinfulness and the necessity of divine judgment. It also reminded them of God's sovereignty and the promise of future restoration.

Do you need a fresh vision of God?

Perhaps, as for Ezekiel, life has not turned out as you had anticipated or hoped. Perhaps a tragedy has left you asking questions similar to those of the Jews: Where is God? Why doesn't he intervene? Does he really care?

We have time to look at only selected passages from this book, but take heart as you glimpse Ezekiel's vision of the future. And look forward to even more. The reality that God has in store for us is greater than the prophet could ever have imagined. Ezekiel points us forward to a far greater salvation. He points us to Christ, who opens up heaven for us.

So keep on serving through turbulent times, keep on trusting God's sovereignty and keep striving for holiness with the Spirit's power.

We are almost there.

Day 1

Read Ezekiel 1:1–28
Key verses: Ezekiel 1:25–28

....

²⁵ Then there came a voice from above the vault over their heads as they stood with lowered wings. ²⁶ Above the vault over their heads was what looked like a throne of lapis lazuli, and high above on the throne was a figure like that of a man. ²⁷ I saw that from what appeared to be his waist up he looked like glowing metal, as if full of fire, and that from there down he looked like fire; and brilliant light surrounded him. ²⁸ Like the appearance of a rainbow in the clouds on a rainy day, so was the radiance around him.

This was the appearance of the likeness of the glory of the LORD. When I saw it, I fell face down, and I heard the voice of one speaking.

Have you ever been speechless?

When Ezekiel had a vision of the glory of God – the visible manifestation of God's presence – he was lost for words.

He repeats phrases like 'what looked like' and 'the appearance of', straining at imagery to convey the splendour of God.

First, he sees the Lord, the divine warrior, riding in a storm, surrounded by fire and lightning (verse 4). Storms and lightning are often associated with theophanies, appearances of God, in the Bible.

Next he notices the cherubim (verses 5–14). They have four faces: the face of a human being, the highest of God's creation; the face of a lion, the highest wild animal; the face of an ox, the highest domestic animal; and the face of an eagle, the highest bird. These cherubim embody the highest attributes of creation. They are the guardians of God's holiness, his heavenly bodyguard. They are the ones that keep Isaiah away in the temple, crying, 'Holy, holy, holy.' The cherubim are also God's law-enforcers. They stand at the gate of the Garden of Eden with their swords drawn, barring the way back into God's presence for those who have rebelled. Their presence is a sign that God is going to judge his people. But, as in Genesis, the rainbow (verse 28) signals that in his wrath God will remember mercy.

And at the centre of the vision, God, in human form, sits on the throne.

Ezekiel fell on his face before God.

There is no other adequate response.

As you look at what is happening around the world, in your church and in your personal life, perhaps you're asking the same question as the exiles: 'Where is God?' Like them, we desperately need a fresh vision of God. Reread Ezekiel's vision, be still in God's presence and pray for a renewed appreciation of his glory. Physically and spiritually bow low before him. Remember, God is still on the throne. Acknowledge his sovereignty over world affairs and all the details of your life. And watch out – seeing God's glory always makes an impact. As happened with Moses, our faces will shine when we have spent time in God's holy presence.

Day 2

Read Ezekiel 1:1–28
Key verses: Ezekiel 1:19–21

....

¹⁹When the living creatures moved, the wheels beside them moved; and when the living creatures rose from the ground, the wheels also rose. ²⁰Wherever the spirit would go, they would go, and the wheels would rise along with them, because the spirit of the living creatures was in the wheels. ²¹When the creatures moved, they also moved; when the creatures stood still, they also stood still; and when the creatures rose from the ground, the wheels rose along with them, because the spirit of the living creatures was in the wheels.

What did the vision mean?

The storm that races across the desert, the living creatures with their legs and their wings, the wheels within wheels spinning around – all of this describes a scene of motion, action and speed. The point is that the Lion of Judah is not caged back in Jerusalem. He is restless and marching around with Ezekiel and all the other exiles in Babylon.

Ezekiel describes a massive war chariot, with one exception: normally a chariot can move only forwards and backwards. This chariot is multi-directional – it can move forwards, backwards, upwards, downwards and sideways. It can move in any direction it wants to, at the speed of light or faster. Verses 20–21 tell us why: because it is driven by the Spirit of God. 'Wherever the spirit would go, they would go.'

God wanted to encourage and warn the Israelites that he was God over the whole earth and was with them wherever they went. He was sovereign just as much in Babylon as he was in Jerusalem. He was with them where they were, far from home.

The same Lord who led the exiles out of Egypt and stayed with them in Babylon is Lord of his church today. Jesus says to us, 'I am with you always' (Matthew 28:20). When you go to the office, when you sit by the bedside of a sick loved one, when you travel away from home – God is present with you.

Psalm 139:7 asks, 'Where can I go from your Spirit? Where can I flee from your presence?' The answer is, 'Nowhere!' As we go through the routines of life, deal with suffering and bereavement, go to hospital appointments and job interviews, and witness to friends, Jesus says to us, 'I am with you.' Meditate on Psalm 139 and the promise that, wherever you go today, God will be with you. Grasp the challenge and comfort of this truth. Listen to God's leading, rely on the strength of his Spirit, and look out for his purposes in all your activities and conversations.

Day 3

Read Ezekiel 2:1–10
Key verses: Ezekiel 2:3–5

....

> ³He said: 'Son of man, I am sending you to the Israelites, to a rebellious nation that has rebelled against me; they and their ancestors have been in revolt against me to this very day. ⁴The people to whom I am sending you are obstinate and stubborn. Say to them, "This is what the Sovereign LORD says." ⁵And whether they listen or fail to listen – for they are a rebellious people – they will know that a prophet has been among them.'

Is the Bible a divine book?

Prophecies being fulfilled, salvation history unfolding and key themes weaving their way through the text all point to God's divine authorship.

Notice, for example, the connections between the books of Ezekiel and Revelation. Both begin with a theophany –

an appearance of God in Christ. In Revelation the Lord is walking among the churches; in Ezekiel God is among his people wherever they are. The two books have a similar message and carry a warning from God.

When you glance through Ezekiel chapter 2 you'll find the word 'rebel' and 'rebellious' repeated; that's how God saw his people. No other people had had so much done for them, nor so consistently rejected the Word and the will of God, as these people had. Like a rebellious vassal state they had sided with the enemy instead of their liege Lord (verse 3). They were a disobedient race, a hardened people, who refused to recognize God's sovereignty.

Consequently, Ezekiel's call was not going to be an easy one. He was not being sent like a Wycliffe missionary into an area that had never heard the truth. That would have been an easier job because at least the people would have listened. The Israelites, though they had the Scriptures, though they knew that Ezekiel was God's servant, would not listen to him.

And, as Chris Wright in his commentary points out, 'It is still tragically true that in some parts of the world . . . God's Word receives a better hearing among those who have never heard it than among those established churches who have grown hard and deaf in their resistance to the movements of God's Spirit' (*The Message of Ezekiel*, The Bible Speaks Today, IVP, 2001, p. 57).

Remember Jesus' words repeated through the early chapters of Revelation: 'Whoever has ears, let them hear what the Spirit says to the churches.'

What is God saying to you and your church? Not many of us set out to resist God, but, over time, if we are not listening to him in his Word, his voice will grow faint. Today, listen for God speaking to you and obey all that he tells you to do.

> Everyone who hears these words of mine and puts them into practice is like a wise man who built his house on the rock.
> (Matthew 7:24)

Day 4

Read Ezekiel 3:1–19

Key verses: Ezekiel 3:11, 17

^{...}

¹¹ Go now to your people in exile and speak to them. Say to them, 'This is what the Sovereign L<small>ORD</small> says,' whether they listen or fail to listen . . . ¹⁷ Son of man, I have made you a watchman for the people of Israel; so hear the word I speak and give them warning from me.

Do you feel called by God?

Some Christians have a very clear sense that God has called them to a particular career or ministry. Ezekiel was called by God, but his was a call we all share regardless of our job title, age or stage of life.

God called Ezekiel to take his Word seriously and live a life of compliant obedience to that Word. Specifically he was called to be:

• A spokesman

Like all prophets, Ezekiel couldn't decide his own message, audience or how his words would be received. He was to consume the Word of God (3:1), absorb the Word into the totality of his life, and then proclaim it.

We too have been given a book that we are to inwardly digest. We have not been given a blank sheet on which we can write our own message, but a book with writing on every page, with no room for additions (2:9). And we are to proclaim its message. This will be a bittersweet experience, because although the Word tastes sweet as it thrills our hearts and satisfies our souls, it is an unpopular message many will reject.

• A watchman

Ezekiel's job was to remind the people that judgment was coming. God's wrath against all the ungodliness and unrighteousness of men and women was soon to be revealed. Many other prophets in Ezekiel and Jeremiah's day fudged the issue of judgment (Jeremiah 6:13–14). There is a temptation for us to do the same – to sugar-coat the gospel so we only talk about God's love. But we are called to be watchmen, urging people to flee from the coming wrath. We need to tell people the bad news as well as the good news. As the American pastor and author Tim Keller explains: 'We are more wicked than we ever dared believe, but more loved and accepted in Christ than we ever dared hope' ('More Wicked But More Loved', 4 February 2015, <dailykeller.com>).

We don't all have the gift of evangelism, but we are all spokespeople and watchmen. That means being ready and willing to share the gospel, the difficult truth as well as the good news, not just through the witness of our lives but with words as well. Don't dwell on the rejection you may face: that is part of the job description. The prophets, apostles and even Jesus himself faced rejection. Instead be motivated by the urgency of the task and the privilege of introducing people to Jesus. Today, look out for opportunities to share your faith. Pray that your words would be full of truth, compassion and hope.

Day 5

Read Ezekiel 2:1–2; 3:8–15
Key verses: Ezekiel 2:2; 3:12, 14

....

> ² As he spoke, the Spirit came into me and raised me
> to my feet, and I heard him speaking to me . . .
> ³:¹² Then the Spirit lifted me up, and I heard behind
> me a loud rumbling sound as the glory of the Lᴏʀᴅ
> rose from the place where it was standing . . . ¹⁴ The
> Spirit then lifted me up and took me away, and I
> went in bitterness and in the anger of my spirit, with
> the strong hand of the Lᴏʀᴅ on me.

Have you ever had a 'mountain top' experience of God? Some special encounter with him, perhaps in your quiet time or during a worship service at church?

These times are precious but they are not an end in themselves. I imagine Ezekiel might have preferred to lie there on the ground, awed by his majestic vision of God. But it isn't paralysis that God wants; it is reasonable service.

Ezekiel is not on his knees for very long before the Spirit comes and enables him to stand up. Notice how central the Spirit of God is to this vision. It is the Spirit who raises Ezekiel to his feet, strengthens him, makes him as tough as his opponents, deposits him among the exiles, puts him in the place of service and equips him for the task.

It is interesting that Ezekiel couldn't even stand up without the Spirit lifting him (2:1). Perhaps like many Old Testament prophets he was reluctant to step out in service. He needed God's equipping and enabling. Yet we seem to be able to stand up, preach, plan, counsel and minister without the Spirit! In practice our theology is one of self-reliance, whereas God wants us to rely on him.

If God speaks to you from his Word, he is speaking to you so he might push you into service. And he equips you for the ministry to which he calls you. He gives his Spirit to strengthen and enable you.

Don't serve in your own strength; rely on his.

Stop. You can't do everything in your own strength – raising your children, serving in church, being faithful at work, looking after others. God's plan was never to save you by grace and then make you live by your own efforts. You have the ever-present, ever-ready, eternal

God living within you – listen to him and lean on him. He is your guarantee of glory, assurance of salvation, comforter, counsellor, guide, sanctifier, advocate in prayer and giver of gifts for service. Invite the Holy Spirit to direct every action and give wisdom for every conversation today. Walk through your days in tandem with him and see his fruit more and more on display in your life (Galatians 5:22–25).

Day 6

Read Ezekiel 2:1 – 3:10
Key verses: Ezekiel 3:1–4

••

¹*And he said to me, 'Son of man, eat what is before you, eat this scroll; then go and speak to the people of Israel.'* ²*So I opened my mouth, and he gave me the scroll to eat.*

³*Then he said to me, 'Son of man, eat this scroll I am giving you and fill your stomach with it.' So I ate it, and it tasted as sweet as honey in my mouth.*

⁴*He then said to me: 'Son of man, go now to the people of Israel and speak my words to them.'*

Do you have a nickname? A name given by friends and family that highlights one of your particular character traits?

In chapters 2 and 3 God repeatedly calls Ezekiel 'son of man', emphasizing his humanity and mortality.

God will accomplish his work among the exiles through a son of man – one who obeys his Word and is committed to suffering whatever God sends along his path in order to accomplish God's will. Have you heard that anywhere else in the Bible? I think this is one of the reasons why Jesus prefers the title 'Son of Man' in the Gospels. He is fulfilling Daniel's vision of the heavenly being and also this image in Ezekiel of the 'son of man' who suffers, serves and speaks the Word of God. Ultimately God was going to accomplish his purpose through Jesus, the Son of Man, who would come into the world.

Ezekiel's imagery and metaphors are used not just in the Gospels, but also in the book of Revelation. In chapter 1 John sees a similar vision: one like a son of man, dressed in a robe reaching down to his feet, with a golden sash around his chest, his head and hair white as snow and eyes like blazing fire. He is seeing the Lord Jesus on his throne.

Like the prophet Ezekiel we are to bring God glory through faithful obedience. We are to listen to and speak God's words regardless of the obstacles, confident we are following in Jesus' footsteps. Draw strength from the one who has finished the work God gave him to do and is now seated on heaven's throne in sovereign power.

Jesus has gone before us, blazing a trail, the ultimate Son of Man who was obedient to his Father in every way. Imagine yourself following his footprints as you daily journey on this path of humility, self-denial and God-honouring service. Faithful Christians past and present are cheering you on. Jesus is waiting for you at the finish line. Keep your eyes focused on him and ask the Holy Spirit for renewed strength to run the particular race God has set for you.

> Do you see what this means – all these pioneers who blazed the way, all these veterans cheering us on? It means we'd better get on with it. Strip down, start running – and never quit! No extra spiritual fat, no parasitic sins. Keep your eyes on *Jesus*, who both began and finished this race we're in. Study how he did it. Because he never lost sight of where he was headed – that exhilarating finish in and with God – he could put up with anything along the way: Cross, shame, whatever. And now he's *there*, in the place of honor, right alongside God. When you find yourselves flagging in your faith, go over that story again, item by item, that long litany of hostility he plowed through. *That* will shoot adrenaline into your souls!
> (Hebrews 12:1–3, MSG)

Day 7

Read Ezekiel 8:1–18
Key verses: Ezekiel 8:9–12

. . . .

> [9] *And he said to me, 'Go in and see the wicked and detestable things they are doing here' . . . and I saw portrayed all over the walls all kinds of crawling things and unclean animals and all the idols of Israel.* [11] *In front of them stood seventy elders of Israel . . . Each had a censer in his hand, and a fragrant cloud of incense was rising.*
>
> [12] *He said to me, 'Son of man, have you seen what the elders of Israel are doing in the darkness, each at the shrine of his own idol? They say, "The LORD does not see us; the LORD has forsaken the land."'*

It is uncomfortable to think God is angry with his people.

Ezekiel had been using symbols to show the people that, because of their sin, the wrath of God was coming; and they didn't like it. One day the exiled elders of Judah visited Ezekiel hoping he would have a new message:

that Jerusalem would be safe and that God would rescue them. Being so far away from home they found it tempting to pin all their hopes on the future of the city of Jerusalem.

Suddenly, as they were talking, Ezekiel was swept up into a vision. He was taken from Babylon on a virtual reality tour round the temple in Jerusalem so he could understand why God was so angry and why destruction was coming.

The first scene takes place outside the temple where the goddess Asherah was being worshipped, involving all kinds of sexual immorality. Then the tour moves progressively closer to the heart of the temple precincts. We see the elders, key people from the community, worshipping the Egyptian gods. In case the Egyptians won the power struggle with the Babylonians, these businessmen were looking after their interests and garnering Egyptian goodwill. The elders' assumption was that, as God had deserted them, they needed other sources of help. The women also, in verses 14–15, were weeping for Tammuz, a Babylonian god of nature, at the north gate of the temple itself.

Like a betrayed lover God was jealous. He was angry that his covenant people had become idolaters, worshipping false gods.

Are we idolaters?

If we sacrifice relationships to win the blessing of the god 'career', we are idolaters. If we squander the precious hours of our lives for the god of 'entertainment', we are idolaters. If we crave the self-affirmation we get from sex or power, we are idolaters. If our self-worth is measured by our net worth, we are idolaters.

And God is jealous.

Ask the Holy Spirit to reveal where, consciously or unconsciously, someone or something has taken God's place in your life. Has career, family, money or image become a false god? Reflect on God's faithfulness to you in the past; return to your 'first love'; and get back into the spiritual habits you practised when you were passionate about Christ: Bible study, prayer and whole-hearted service (Revelation 2:4–5).

Day 8

Read Ezekiel 8:1–18
Key verses: Ezekiel 8:16–17

....

> ¹⁶*He then brought me into the inner court of the house of the LORD, and there at the entrance to the temple, between the portico and the altar, were about twenty-five men. With their backs towards the temple of the LORD and their faces towards the east, they were bowing down to the sun in the east.*
>
> ¹⁷*He said to me, 'Have you seen this, son of man? Is it a trivial matter for the people of Judah to do the detestable things they are doing here?'*

You can't have your cake and eat it!

But that is exactly what the Israelites were trying to do.

From verse 16 onwards, Ezekiel is taken into the heart of the temple, reserved for the priests and Levites, immediately in front of the Most Holy Place. In that sacred spot where God is worshipped the people are bowing with their bottoms up to the Most Holy Place and their heads down to the rising sun coming from the east.

The Israelites hadn't stopped worshipping the God of Israel. They were just not sure they could get by with his help alone, so they were covering themselves, politically and spiritually. They were prepared to worship God as long as their worship was modified by the new realities of life in which the gods of Babylon were strong.

Notice, God does not make any comment when the Canaanites worship their Canaanite gods or the people of Babylon worship their Babylonian gods. But he is provoked to jealousy when his people, who believe that he is the God who has acted in the past, prostitute themselves to other idols. He is angered when his own people want a private faith but also want publicly to admit that anti-God ideas, accepted by society, have won the day.

The message of chapter 8 is that we must be intolerant of idolatry among ourselves. God will not be treated simply as one option among many.

Are you trying to have your cake and eat it? Sometimes we don't even realize it, but we allow our money, health, reputation, family, even our role in church, to be a security blanket – an extra layer of comfort, another source of value and esteem. Check your heart: are you idolizing these things? Our sovereign God does not need to be, and will not tolerate being, one option among many. Take time to meditate on Paul's charge:

> Don't let the world around you squeeze you into its own mould, but let God re-mould your minds from within, so that you may prove in practice that the plan of God for you is good, meets all his demands and moves towards the goal of true maturity.
>
> (Romans 12:2, PHILLIPS)

Day 9

Read Ezekiel 9:1–11
Key verses: Ezekiel 9:8–10

．．

⁸*While they were killing and I was left alone, I fell face down, crying out, 'Alas, Sovereign LORD! Are you going to destroy the entire remnant of Israel in this outpouring of your wrath on Jerusalem?'*

⁹He answered me, 'The sin of the people of Israel and Judah is exceedingly great; the land is full of bloodshed and the city is full of injustice. They say, "The LORD has forsaken the land; the LORD does not see." ¹⁰So I will not look on them with pity or spare them, but I will bring down on their own heads what they have done.'

People say there can't be a God because a good God would put an end to the evil in the world.

God is patient, but he does not shut his eyes to human sin. He is not indifferent. Judgment cannot be held back for ever.

For centuries various kings of Israel and Judah had come along and led the people into one idolatrous action after another. But in chapter 9 Ezekiel has a vision of God's intervention. And judgment begins, not with the unbeliever, but with the believer (1 Peter 4:17).

Our body is a temple of the Holy Spirit, so we must honour God with it, not pamper it in self-indulgence or abuse it (1 Corinthians 6:19–20). What must God think of the believer who professes to believe in the sovereignty of God on Sunday but every other day looks for worldly solutions to his or her problems? Or the one who swears allegiance to Christ on Sunday but serves the bottom line the rest of the week?

Next, God visits judgment on the church, his covenant people; corporately they too are his temple. What does he think of our half-hearted evangelism, our toying with New Age ideas, our tolerance of old heresies, our questioning of some of the basic truths of the Bible, our elevation of subjective truth over the objective truth of Scripture? What does he think about leaders who deny Jesus' resurrection or who, in an attempt to appear relevant, play down God's judgment and wrath?

God is not indifferent. He will not tolerate this for ever. Judgment is coming.

Meditate on Psalm 51 and confess your sins to God:

Almighty and most merciful Father, we have wandered and strayed from your ways like lost sheep. We have followed too much the devices and desires of our own hearts. We have offended against your holy laws. We have left undone those things that we ought to have done; and we have done those things that we ought not to have done; and there is no health in us. But you, O Lord, have mercy upon us sinners. Spare those who confess their faults. Restore those who are penitent, according to your promises declared to mankind in Christ Jesus our Lord. And grant, O most merciful Father, for his sake, that we may live a disciplined, righteous and godly life, to the glory of your holy name. Amen.

(Prayer of Penitence, *Common Worship: Daily Prayer*, Church House Publishing, 2005)

Day 10

Read Ezekiel 9:1–11
Key verses: Ezekiel 9:3–6

....

> ³ Then the LORD called to the man clothed in linen who had the writing kit at his side ⁴ and said to him, 'Go throughout the city of Jerusalem and put a mark on the foreheads of those who grieve and lament over all the detestable things that are done in it.'
>
> ⁵ As I listened, he said to the others, 'Follow him through the city and kill, without showing pity or compassion. ⁶ Slaughter the old men, the young men and women, the mothers and children, but do not touch anyone who has the mark.'

Can we escape God's final, inevitable judgment?

Only if we have the mark of God on us.

In Ezekiel's vision the angel is commanded to go through the city putting a mark on the foreheads of those who grieve and lament over the detestable state of the nation. Those with the mark are saved from God's judgment.

Revelation 7:3 talks about the mark, the seal of God, on the foreheads of the servants of the Lord. These were people with a broken and contrite spirit who wept over the sin of their church and nation. They repudiated the standards of the people around them. Like Daniel, there was no spirit of criticism in them (see Daniel 9). They were not coming to God saying, 'Do something about those sinful people.' They were saying, 'Forgive me for my sin.'

Remember also that protective mark, the dab of blood from the Passover lamb, put on the doors of Hebrew homes as the angel of death came to visit (Exodus 12:12–13). In the Bible's larger storyline, the mercy of God in the midst of judgment finds its ultimate expression in the person of Jesus Christ. His blood shed on the cross saves us from the coming wrath.

Turn to Jesus to find refuge from God's wrath. Only his blood shed on the cross can wash away your sin, remove your guilt and appease God's anger. Don't seek security in other people or things; don't try to save yourself through effort and good works; don't be so distracted by other people's sins that you don't repent of your own. Let Jesus' blood cleanse you and mark you out as a child of his grace. Today, thank God that you are headed for heaven, dressed in robes of righteousness, with his name written on you (Revelation 9:4; 14:1; 22:4).

Day 11

Read Ezekiel 10:1–22
Key verses: Ezekiel 10:4–5, 18

···

> ⁴*Then the glory of the* LORD *rose from above the cherubim and moved to the threshold of the temple. The cloud filled the temple, and the court was full of the radiance of the glory of the* LORD. ⁵*The sound of the wings of the cherubim could be heard as far away as the outer court, like the voice of God Almighty when he speaks . . .*
>
> ¹⁸*Then the glory of the* LORD *departed from over the threshold of the temple and stopped above the cherubim.*

They never believed it would happen.

The Jews never believed that Judah and Jerusalem would be devastated because they didn't think God would abandon the temple. Jeremiah had mocked the people for their false confidence. They kept repeating, 'The temple of the LORD', as if by simply saying this mantra they would be supernaturally protected from danger (Jeremiah 7:4).

But, shocking though it might be, the city falls. God is moving somewhere else (9:3). The winged chariot begins to move (10:4–5); the glory of the Lord departs from the threshold of the temple (10:18); it leaves the city and rests above the mountain (11:22–24).

God has made his message clear. He is not a God of a place but of people. He is passionately concerned for their spiritual life. He is prepared to sacrifice their reputation, comfort and success if he can bring them back to the place where they are purified, repentant and effective for him again. He is far more concerned about the holiness of his people than about their happiness. His goal is restored relationship with those in exile: 'They will be my people, and I will be their God' (11:20).

God has not changed. He still prioritizes holiness over happiness and is passionately concerned about our spiritual growth. And as John Calvin comments, 'The scourges of God are more useful to us because when God indulges us we abuse his clemency and flatter ourselves and grow hardened in our sin' (quoted in Iain Duguid, *Ezekiel*, NIV Application Commentary, Zondervan, 1999, p. 115).

Christian people don't do well in good days. We grow fat, flabby and lazy. We need preaching that challenges what we are pinning our hopes on, where our priorities lie and all the other idolatries of our day.

Just as God purges a people, so he disciplines us as individuals. See this discipline of God for what it really is – not evidence he has abandoned you, but proof of his love. Don't waste your suffering, but use this time of being laid low to grow in your faith. Draw close to God, acknowledge your dependence on him, trust him for all that is to come, thank him for his grace and mercy, and allow him to purify you.

> Consider it pure joy, my brothers and sisters, whenever you face trials of many kinds, because you know that the testing of your faith produces perseverance. Let perseverance finish its work so that you may be mature and complete, not lacking anything.
> (James 1:2–4)

Day 12

Read Ezekiel 11:1–25
Key verses: Ezekiel 11:22–23

....

²² Then the cherubim, with the wheels beside them, spread their wings, and the glory of the God of Israel was above them. ²³ The glory of the LORD went up from within the city and stopped above the mountain east of it.

Do you have a 'special' place? Somewhere you keep returning to, somewhere that holds precious memories?

The Mount of Olives is a special location in the Bible, simply because of the number of times God visits it.

At the end of chapter 11 the glory departs from Jerusalem and hovers above the Mount of Olives, just east of the city. Remember, five hundred years later, the glory of God was going to be visiting the temple again – this time not as a cloud of fire, not with cherubim, but in a person: 'We have seen his glory, the glory of the one and only Son, who came from the Father, full of grace and truth' (John 1:14). The glory of God revisits the temple twice and on both occasions he clears the temple. He is looking for righteousness, and finds unrighteousness; for holiness, and finds sinfulness; for true worship, and finds a den of thieves.

The glory comes and the glory leaves, pausing at the city gate to be stripped, scorned, ill-treated and crucified. The glory leaves and pauses again on the Mount of Olives, to give his last words to his church to go into all the world. His people are to spread the gospel through-out the whole world. People from every tribe and tongue and nation are to be gathered under his kingship.

On that mountain he promised to be with his people to the ends of the earth. That presence can be found wherever his people are, even when they find themselves exiled in a strange land. And to that Mount of Olives he will come again, in power and glory; when 'the kingdom of the world has become the kingdom of our Lord and of his Messiah, and he will reign for ever and ever', and every creature, the cherubim and the redeemed, will sing, 'Hallelujah! For our Lord God Almighty reigns' (Revelation 11:15; 19:6).

One day soon, perhaps today, Jesus will return to the Mount of Olives. His second coming will be very different from his first. He will come in power, majesty and glory; everyone will bow before him and confess him as Lord (Philippians 2:10–11). Until then, let Jesus' last words on the mountain shape your priorities, and encourage, reassure and spur you to action: 'Go and make disciples of all nations . . . I am with you always, to the very end of the age' (Matthew 28:19–20).

Day 13

Read Ezekiel 34:1–10
Key verses: Ezekiel 34:4–5, 10

....

> *⁴You have not strengthened the weak or healed those who are ill or bound up the injured. You have not brought back the strays or searched for the lost. You have ruled them harshly and brutally. ⁵So they were scattered because there was no shepherd, and when they were scattered they became food for all the wild animals . . . ¹⁰I am against the shepherds and will hold them accountable for my flock. I will remove them from tending the flock.*

The world is divided into three camps: those who make things happen, those who watch what's happening and those who have no idea what is happening!

The ones who make things happen are the leaders. Leaders can do a power of good, but those corrupted by power are a menace. God addresses Israel's corrupted leaders in chapter 34. He uses the title 'shepherd', a very familiar one in the ancient world, a metaphor for the king or god of a state or country. This title was always used to emphasize the responsibility of those in power to enforce social righteousness.

The Lord is angry with these former kings of Judah because they failed to fulfil their role as shepherds. Of course, these shepherds did not own the flock; they were employed as stewards to look after the sheep, answerable to the Chief Shepherd. Notice that God repeatedly calls his people 'my sheep'.

Nevertheless, the monarchy of Israel was responsible for much of the nation's apostasy. They introduced idolatry, they arranged foreign alliances, trusting foreign powers to protect and provide for them instead of God, and they enforced harsh rule which threatened the reputation of God, who was known as compassionate and merciful.

And because of the absence of a true shepherd, the people of God had been scattered. God holds the kings responsible for tearing the tribes of Israel apart – ten in the north, two in the south, and in constant warfare with each other.

Ezekiel warns that, because of the shepherds' sinful self-interest, judgment is coming on them. They now face a greater enemy than any they have ever fought: the Lord himself.

Many of us have leadership responsibilities – as a small-group leader, parent, manager or employer. Do you see your leadership as a status symbol or a boost to your ego? Do you use people for your own convenience? Sometimes our motives are mixed and the influence that comes with our role corrupts our hearts. Today, take a spiritual health check. Ask God to point out areas of sinful self-interest, circumstances where you are not trusting him fully or times you failed to represent him well to his people. Avoid God's judgment: repent and return to the Chief Shepherd.

Day 14

Read Ezekiel 34:11–24
Key verses: Ezekiel 34:12, 14

....

> [12]*As a shepherd looks after his scattered flock when he is with them, so will I look after my sheep. I will rescue them from all the places where they were scattered on a day of clouds and darkness . . .* [14]*I will tend them in a good pasture, and the mountain heights of Israel will be their grazing land. There they will lie down in good grazing land, and there they will feed in a rich pasture on the mountains of Israel.*

What does a true leader look like?

God uses the term 'shepherd' to describe a true leader. We may see the image of a shepherd as a sentimental one. But often in the ancient world a shepherd was regarded as more of a cowboy: tender with his sheep; tough in the way he had to live.

God promises the people a coming shepherd who will be tough and tender, one who will gather the scattered nations. 'I will search for the lost and bring back the strays,' says the Lord (verse 16). You hear that again on the lips of Jesus, who says, 'The Son of Man came to seek and to save the lost' (Luke 19:10). Isaiah 40:11 gives us this description of the Lord our Shepherd: 'He gathers the lambs in his arms and carries them close to his heart; he gently leads those that have young.' In contrast to Israel's previous kings, the Lord can be trusted not to scatter the flock; to teach and not deceive; to feed and not fleece the flock.

This idea of the shepherd feeding and tending the flock is taken up in the New Testament and used of leadership within local churches. Paul describes the role of the Ephesian elders: 'Keep watch over . . . all the flock of which the Holy Spirit has made you overseers. Be shepherds of the church of God, which he bought with his own blood' (Acts 20:28). The rest of Acts 20 indicates that this means testifying to the gospel of God's grace, warning people day and night with tears and proclaiming the whole counsel of God. You feed people by telling them the Word of God, sharing about a judgment that's coming and the love of God that can rescue them from it.

If you have a responsibility in your local church, whatever level it is, you are a shepherd of God's flock. Fulfil that calling willingly (1 Peter 5:2–3). Make sure you are doing it to serve people. You are there to care for, woo and win them. Love God's people. Love them to death; love them into the kingdom: that's the role of the shepherd.

How would you rate yourself as a leader? Don't be tempted to adopt the world's criteria to judge how you are getting on. The role of God's shepherd is to care for the spiritual, material and emotional needs of the flock. Today, be quick to demonstrate servant leadership, to value people as individuals and outdo yourself in showing love (1 Peter 1:22; 4:8).

Day 15

Read Ezekiel 34:11–24
Key verses: Ezekiel 34:15–16

....

[15] I myself will tend my sheep and make them lie down, declares the Sovereign LORD. [16] I will search for the lost and bring back the strays. I will bind up the injured and strengthen the weak, but the sleek and the strong I will destroy. I will shepherd the flock with justice.

What is God's solution to a history of bad shepherds?

Ezekiel points further into the future and explains that God will change not the nature of the office, but the nature of the occupant. God will replace the bad shepherds with a good shepherd: someone like David, a king after God's own heart.

Who is this shepherd? Psalm 23 says, 'The LORD is my shepherd.' The New Testament unfolds this answer even further. Jesus says, 'I am the good shepherd' (John 10:11).

Jesus was actually basing what he was saying on this passage from Ezekiel and it was a radical thing to say. His listeners were shaken and questioned whether he was demon-possessed or raving mad (John 10:19). They later picked up rocks to throw at him (John 10:31). What was it about this title that provoked such an extreme reaction?

Jesus knew exactly what he was saying when he called himself the 'good shepherd'. He was saying that Herod, king of Judah, was not a true king. But more than that, he was calling himself by the title used for God himself.

Jesus was separating himself from all the other kings, messianic pretenders and freedom fighters who called themselves 'shepherds' and were trying to unite the people behind their goal of driving out the Romans. The violent methods of these revolutionaries meant many following these shepherds were killed. Jesus reminds the people that, in contrast to these leaders, he has their interests at heart, he loves them and he will lay down his life for them.

Jesus comes as the one shepherd who will unite the flock; there will be one flock and one shepherd (John 10:16). He is the good shepherd who will look for the one lost sheep (Luke 15:3–7). He is the discerning shepherd who, in the final judgment, will separate the sheep from the goats (Matthew 25:31–46, again using Ezekiel 34 language). And when it comes to his church, he is the Chief Shepherd to whom all the under-shepherds report (1 Peter 5:4). Jesus is the fulfilment of all God's promises to King David: the ultimate Shepherd-King.

Politicians, celebrities, even some church leaders, parade as shepherds, claiming to have your best interests at heart while using your allegiance to build their personal empire and reputation. But Jesus is the only one who loves you enough to lay down his life for you. He is your Shepherd-King who alone provides protection, refreshment, guidance, satisfaction, comfort and support. Meditate on the truths of Psalm 23. Listen for your Shepherd's voice and determine to follow wherever he leads.

Day 16

Read Ezekiel 34:25–31

Key verses: Ezekiel 34:25–26, 28

. . . .

²⁵*I will make a covenant of peace with them and rid the land of savage beasts so that they may live in the wilderness and sleep in the forests in safety.* ²⁶*I will make them and the places surrounding my hill a blessing. I will send down showers in season; there will be showers of blessing . . .* ²⁸*They will no longer be plundered by the nations, nor will wild animals devour them. They will live in safety, and no one will make them afraid.*

What difference will Jesus' coming make?

In place of the curses of the Sinai covenant that the Israelites had experienced under the judgment of God – wild animals, drought, famine, the sword – they are now going to experience safety, rain in its season, fruitfulness and peace; *shalom* will reign.

That Hebrew word *shalom*, peace, is much more than simply the cessation of warfare and the absence of strife. It conveys a comprehensive state of wholeness and well-being. It suggests a people who are free from fear and insecurity and at peace with themselves; a people who have a relationship with God – the hostility has been resolved and they are reconciled to him; and a people who are also reconciled to nature.

Many of us are afraid of storms, street crime, what other people think, failure, economic downturn, poverty, old age, sickness, bereavement, death. When Jesus comes into our world he is saying, 'I've come to deal with those basic fundamental fears and insecurities that lie at the very core of your human nature. I've come to bring peace right into the heart of your life. I've come to bring a peace that the world cannot give or take away.' That's why Ezekiel promises that when the king comes there will be no fear at any time and no-one to make them afraid (verse 28). The good shepherd defines the measure of the *shalom*: 'I have come that they may have life, and have it to the full' (John 10:10).

The *shalom* of God is not an activity or an afternoon of undisturbed dozing; it is not boring – there is no need for you to look at your watch when you're enjoying this peace. It is a life where every minute satisfies, every second is worth savouring, where each hour has new pleasures; a life where activity is fulfilling and every sensation brings pleasure.

Being reconciled to God means that you enjoy a restored relationship with him. This is real, everlasting, not-dependent-on-feelings peace. Don't let fears or anxieties rob you of this peace. Instead bring your prayer requests to God. Invite him to minister his *shalom* to your heart and mind (Philippians 4:6–7).

May the Lord of peace himself give you peace at all times and in every way.
(2 Thessalonians 3:16)

Day 17

Read Ezekiel 34:25–31

Key verses: Ezekiel 34:29–30

. . . .

[29] I will provide for them a land renowned for its crops, and they will no longer be victims of famine in the land or bear the scorn of the nations. [30] Then they will know that I, the LORD their God, am with them and that they, the Israelites, are my people, declares the Sovereign LORD.

The Bible is full of promises.

Here, Ezekiel speaks of a renewed covenant, at the heart of which is this wonderful promise of God: the Lord is your God and you are his people. Instead of having a monarchy divided by sin, God's people will be united under one shepherd. Instead of an undistinguished succession of monarchs, there will be a single ruler after God's own heart.

Christians experience the blessings of this covenant in a different way from those who lived under the old covenant. One of the things we need to remember is that, in the Old Testament, many of the promises of God are put in terms that the people then would understand. For example, the people of God then had a particular relationship to the land in which they lived. It was God's land, they were his tenants, and the fertility of that land was very often a spiritual thermometer, as Chris Wright puts it, of the relationship between Israel and their God (quoted by Iain Duguid in *Ezekiel*, NIV Application Commentary, Zondervan, 1999, p. 354). So the blessings of God are often described in terms of the fertility of the land.

But Israel failed miserably in their duties. Time and again they broke the terms of their relationship to God. Ezekiel talked about Israel as a vine that was not producing the fruit that God was looking for. But when Jesus, the new ruler, came under the new covenant, he said, 'I am the true vine' (John 15:1).

The whole message of the New Testament is about the perfect obedience of Christ in our place. He makes peace by the blood of his cross, so even though we are covenant-breakers by nature, we can have every spiritual blessing in Christ. Through his death on the cross, those who were far away and those who were near are brought together into one new man, all by Christ in this new covenant.

Jesus keeps God's covenant on our behalf, so 'no matter how many promises God has made, they are "Yes" in Christ' (2 Corinthians 1:20). Thank God for being the great promise-keeper. Worship Jesus for dying in your place. Ask the Holy Spirit to help you keep your part of this new covenant relationship today.

> May the God of peace, who through the blood of the eternal covenant brought back from the dead our Lord Jesus, that great Shepherd of the sheep, equip you with everything good for doing his will, and may he work in us what is pleasing to him, through Jesus Christ, to whom be glory for ever and ever. Amen.
> (Hebrews 13:20–21)

Day 18

Read Ezekiel 34:1–31

Key verse: Ezekiel 34:31

....

31 You are my sheep, the sheep of my pasture, and I am your God, declares the Sovereign LORD.

An engagement ring symbolizes a real relationship but with the promise of more to come. Similarly, there is an 'already but not yet' aspect to the new covenant.

The peace we enjoy today is real but partial, because we still live in a fallen world. We experience trials of one kind or another; we still know moments of panic, hours of boredom and days when we struggle with pain. Sometimes these are the results of our foolish choices; at other times, they are not. Sometimes obedience results in material blessing; sometimes it results in persecution, hardship and loss.

Yet even here in the midst of sin, trials and temptation, we can experience inexpressible joy because of the nearness of the Shepherd. We see the blessings in part, though not in fullness. Creation around us still longs for the revelation of the new heavens and the new earth. These light and momentary troubles of ours are nothing in comparison with the glory that awaits us in Christ.

One day, when Christ returns, all of this will be gloriously and fully fulfilled as God gathers together his worldwide flock from many nations and brings them into his presence. There will be no more suffering, no more pain, and no more disharmony with God, my neighbour or even with the world around me (Isaiah 11:6–9).

The Lamb of God, sacrificed in our place, has become our Shepherd-King. Make every effort to stay close to him. Feed on his Word, listen for his voice, accept his protection and put your trust in him. Keep serving, keep fighting sin, keep pursuing righteousness and keep your focus on glory, because the wait is almost over. One day soon, perhaps today, the engagement will culminate in the marriage supper of the Lamb.

For the Lamb at the centre of the throne
  will be their shepherd;
'he will lead them to springs of living water.'
  'And God will wipe away every tear from their eyes.'
(Revelation 7:17)

And when the Chief Shepherd appears, you will receive the crown of glory that will never fade away.

(1 Peter 5:4)

Day 19

Read Ezekiel 36:16–32
Key verses: Ezekiel 36:18–21

....

> [18] *So I poured out my wrath on them because they had shed blood in the land and because they had defiled it with their idols.* [19] *I dispersed them among the nations, and they were scattered through the countries; I judged them according to their conduct and their actions.* [20] *And wherever they went among the nations they profaned my holy name, for it was said of them, 'These are the* LORD*'s people, and yet they had to leave his land.'* [21] *I had concern for my holy name, which the people of Israel profaned among the nations where they had gone.*

The Bible talks about it, preachers teach about it, but what does it really mean to be holy? In the Old Testament, if something was dedicated for God's use, it was said to be holy. So, for example, certain foods and garments were holy because they were used exclusively in God's service (1 Samuel 21:4; Leviticus 16:4).

In the ancient world of Israel people understood the concepts of holiness and ceremonial cleanness. Not only were certain things you ate clean or unclean, but also there were clean lands and unclean lands.

In this chapter, what God is saying to the Israelites is that, even while they were living in the holy land, the clean land, they were desecrating it by their behaviour and idolatry. They were turning it into a place of death, making it a place unfit to live in. Instead of staying away from the thing that was defiled, they had become defiled by it (verse 17). They were acting as if they belonged to the unholy lands of the Gentiles (verse 19). And so God says, 'You want to live as if you're not God's chosen holy people? Then I'll send you out among the unholy, unchosen ones, to live the way you are really living!'

Not only were the people defiled and needing to be cleansed, they were also disobedient and needing to be reconciled to God (verses 26–28). The story of Israel, from the moment of their rescue from Egypt to their settlement in the Promised Land, right up to Ezekiel's time, is one of constant disobedience to God.

The whole story of their history is one of entrenched disobedience to God.

God's rebuke to the Israelites pierces our hearts sharply too. How often have we been guilty of not living as the holy people of God? Rather than live distinctive lives we prefer to blend in with the culture and its values. It's understandable – it is hard to be different – but it is so far from the calling God has in mind for us. Ask God to show you specific areas where your lifestyle and choices reflect the culture so that you are not the salt and light God designed us to be.

Day 20

Read Ezekiel 36:24–36
Key verses: Ezekiel 36:25–27

....

> 25 I will sprinkle clean water on you, and you will be clean; I will cleanse you from all your impurities and from all your idols. 26 I will give you a new heart and put a new spirit in you; I will remove from you your heart of stone and give you a heart of flesh. 27 And I will put my Spirit in you and move you to follow my decrees and be careful to keep my laws.

A heart transplant is a massive operation. And the Israelites needed one.

In Hebrew the heart is the place where we think, decide and will. The spirit is the life-breath, the driving force, which empowers our hearts. It is our aspirations, attitudes, disposition and motivation. The Israelites needed their hearts and spirits transformed; they needed to think and feel differently; and that's what God promises to do (verse 26).

God's intention is to produce heart obedience in his people. This is a creative act on God's part. The Spirit of God will indwell and recreate them in ways that will change and form their will and their ability to follow God's decrees and to keep God's laws. This was God's original intention when they came into the Promised Land (Leviticus 26:3).

The Israelites were not simply sick and in need of some kind of treatment. They were sinners in need of cleansing, rebels in need of reconciliation with their sovereign, dead and in need of life. They had made themselves totally unfit to inhabit God's land and to exist in God's presence. They were offensive to a holy God – and that is our predicament too (Ephesians 2:3).

It is not simply that we're not making the most of life, not fulfilling our potential as human beings or missing out on the spiritual dimension of our humanity. We are under God's wrath and judgment. What we need is radical new birth. Nothing less than this will do. Simply modifying the parameters of our lives, re-socializing ourselves so we behave better, will not do it. Simply handing someone a list of rules and regulations will certainly not do it. We need to be born again, and that is precisely the good news the gospel proclaims.

We don't really like talking about God's judgment or wrath. It is more palatable to present the gospel as a way of life which provides meaning and purpose. But don't miss the point. Don't sell the gospel short. The good news is that when we were facing God's wrath and could do nothing to save ourselves God took the initiative to save us. Jesus' death on the cross paid the penalty for our sin. God's Spirit now dwells within us, gives us a heart transplant and makes obedience possible. That is truly good news worth rejoicing in and sharing with others.

> You see, at just the right time, when we were still powerless, Christ died for the ungodly. Very rarely will anyone die for a righteous person, though for a good person someone might possibly dare to die. But God demonstrates his own love for us in this: while we were still sinners, Christ died for us.
>
> (Romans 5:6–8)

Day 21

Read Ezekiel 37:1–13
Key verses: Ezekiel 37:1–3

....

> [1] *The hand of the LORD was on me, and he brought me out by the Spirit of the LORD and set me in the middle of a valley; it was full of bones.* [2] *He led me to and fro among them, and I saw a great many bones on the floor of the valley, bones that were very dry.* [3] *He asked me, 'Son of man, can these bones live?'*
> *I said, 'Sovereign LORD, you alone know.'*

Ezekiel is transported to Death Valley.

Chapter 37 is a vivid picture of Israel's predicament from God's perspective. But it is also the human predicament. In many ways this chapter is a dramatic illustration of what chapter 36 has been teaching.

The prophet is introduced to a scene of total death – the remains of a mighty army scattered in the valley where once he had seen the glory of God. He walks to and fro among the bones. This is the ultimate picture of despair and hopelessness. That valley of dry bones is where all our plans for the future end up: those years at university, those years invested in your business, career or family. We are all headed to the place of death.

God asks, 'Can these bones live?' Ezekiel doesn't answer God's question but bats it right back and says, 'You alone know.' In New Testament terms the question would be, 'What can be done for the men and women who are without hope and without God? The people we are trying to win for Christ – our friends and family members – are dead before God; they are in the valley of dry bones. What will God do to bring life to those bones?'

Ezekiel himself points us to the answer. No Jew, especially not a priest, would want to be among the dead as that would bring ritual defilement. But God makes Ezekiel walk to and fro through the valley, rubbing his nose in it. And this was the story of Ezekiel's life: he was absolutely absorbed in the will and work of God in his generation. God calls him 'the son of man', and he serves the work of God, getting utterly defiled, going in and out among these dead people.

This son of man, Ezekiel, is a picture of the Son of Man who comes into our world and exposes himself to all the defilement of our sin for our salvation.

We don't like to think about the valley of death. But maybe we need to dwell on Ezekiel's image for a while to appreciate what we have been saved from (Ephesians 2:1) and the desperate plight our loved ones are still in. The task of evangelism and the need for the Holy Spirit to open blind eyes is urgent. What would our friends say to us if they ended up in hell and we hadn't even warned them? Pray for opportunities to share the good news of the gospel with someone today.

Day 22

Read Ezekiel 37:1–14
Key verses: Ezekiel 37:4–6

....

> ⁴ Then he said to me, 'Prophesy to these bones and say to them, "Dry bones, hear the word of the LORD! ⁵ This is what the Sovereign LORD says to these bones: I will make breath enter you, and you will come to life. ⁶ I will attach tendons to you and make flesh come upon you and cover you with skin; I will put breath in you, and you will come to life. Then you will know that I am the LORD."'

Of all the ridiculous things that we find Ezekiel doing in this book, this has to be the most ridiculous.

God tells Ezekiel, 'Prophesy to these bones and say to them, "Dry bones, hear the word of the LORD!"' God is commanding his servant: 'Preach to the dead! Preach the promise of new life and breath and the knowledge of God.' And so Ezekiel preaches the words God has given him to speak. There's no magic rite, no secret incantation, no conjuring trick – it's just the plain, simple, straight-forward speaking of God's truth. It is the proclamation that makes the difference.

The New Testament uses Ezekiel's picture, describing people as dead in their trespasses and sins. It is a grave-yard out there! Getting people to believe our message is impossible. If new life is going to happen in our nation it is through preaching. God has promised he will bless the preaching of his Word.

And notice that it is the preaching of the Word of God and the action of the Spirit of God which together accomplish resurrection. The proclamation of the Word of God creates the context into which the Holy Spirit is happy to move in power to do his resurrection work in these people's lives. Jesus reminded Nicodemus of this key truth in John 3. He told him he needed to be born again by the water and the Spirit: by the cleansing ministry of the Spirit through the Word that renews.

The real secret of spiritual life for our churches and our nation lies in the Word and the Spirit, by proclamation and prayer.

Meditate today on the power of God's Word and the Holy Spirit.

> For the word of God is alive and active. Sharper than any double-edged sword, it penetrates even to dividing soul and spirit, joints and marrow; it judges the thoughts and attitudes of the heart.
> (Hebrews 4:12)

> You were washed, you were sanctified, you were justified in the name of the Lord Jesus Christ and by the Spirit of our God.
> (1 Corinthians 6:11)

Pray that the truth of God's Word and the power of his Spirit would revive your soul, inspire your obedience and lead you into a deeper experience of God.

Day 23

Read Ezekiel 37:15–28

Key verses: Ezekiel 37:21–23

....

21 This is what the Sovereign LORD says: I will take the Israelites out of the nations where they have gone. I will gather them from all around and bring them back into their own land. 22 I will make them one nation in the land, on the mountains of Israel. There will be one king over all of them and they will never again be two nations or be divided into two kingdoms. 23 They will no longer defile themselves with their idols and vile images or with any of their offences, for I will save them from all their sinful backsliding, and I will cleanse them. They will be my people, and I will be their God.

If we promise someone something – whether it is to babysit their children or to take them out for a meal – we usually have a good idea how and when we will fulfil that promise.

Through Ezekiel God promises to renew the life of his people. But how and when did God fulfil that promise?

Like many Old Testament prophecies this promise has been fulfilled at various levels. The first was when the exiled Jews returned to Jerusalem. They came back to their land, where they experienced spiritual renewal. They rebuilt the city and the temple; they reclaimed the land in response to the prayers of people like Daniel and the preaching ministry of people like Ezra. Yet it wasn't a long-lasting work.

The primary level at which this prophecy of renewal was fulfilled was at Pentecost, when the Spirit of God became an indwelling presence in the hearts of individual believers. The prophecy has also been fulfilled at various points in church history, when God has visited his people at periods we call 'revival'. The Spirit of God has stirred people to pray, and flowing from the prayer and proclamation of the Word a whole community has been transformed by the Word and the Spirit of God.

I believe the prophecy is yet to be fulfilled with respect to Israel. Their hearts are still hard to the gospel. But the apostle Paul suggests a day is coming when the fullness of the Gentiles will have come in and God's mercy will again be directed towards his ancient people.

Of course, this prophecy is going to be ultimately fulfilled when God brings us to the new heavens and the new earth. When Jesus returns God will make us perfect both in body and in soul.

Personal renewal, those times of increased intimacy with God, happen at various times and in various ways in our Christian life. They always start with repentance. But that, as with every part of our salvation, begins with God, who saves and cleanses us. When the gospel message finds a home in our hearts we do not view ourselves in a better light. Rather we see ourselves as the chief of sinners. But we also grow in our understanding that, though we are far worse than we could ever have imagined, we are more loved than we ever dreamed possible.

Today, repent of your sins – the things you have done and the things you have left undone – and pray for God's cleansing. Also rejoice that you are so greatly loved.

Day 24

Read Ezekiel 37:14–28

Key verses: Ezekiel 37:26–28

∙∙

> [26] *I will make a covenant of peace with them; it will be an everlasting covenant. I will establish them and increase their numbers, and I will put my sanctuary among them for ever.* [27] *My dwelling-place will be with them; I will be their God, and they will be my people.* [28] *Then the nations will know that I the* LORD *make Israel holy, when my sanctuary is among them for ever.*

We guard our reputations fiercely. It's important to us that we are well thought of.

God is also keen to guard his reputation and restore the honour of his name. The whole emphasis in these verses is on people knowing that 'I the LORD have spoken, and I will do it' (Ezekiel 36:36; 37:14). Previously God's name had been defiled among the nations, as people said,

'What kind of God is he? Look at these devastated people, dispossessed of their land. What kind of God is the God of Israel that this should happen? He must be a weak God. Our gods, the gods of Babylon and Egypt, are stronger.' But God says, 'I am going to do this work and the Gentile nations are going to see that I have done it' (Ezekiel 36:22–23). Chapter 37 ends with the emphasis that there is only one way of salvation. There is only one shepherd, one ruler, one flock.

All this is good news, not just for the people but for the Lord himself. The crucifixion, resurrection and then exaltation of Jesus; the miracle of new birth in countless lives; the future conversion and ultimate resurrection of the dead – all this will, in the long run, vindicate his name among the nations. The act of salvation through Jesus Christ will, at the end of history, be the very thing that brings greatest glory to God, and that ought not to surprise us, for there is nothing higher than this.

For God to delight in his own perfections is entirely appropriate; to delight in anything less would be idolatry for him. The exaltation of God is the great end of salvation as well as creation.

Exalting God is not just the chief business of heaven; it should be our consuming passion now. How do we exalt God? Every time we choose to do his will rather than our own, every time we give him the praise he is due, every time we advance his cause, we are exalting God. Today, look for opportunities to exalt God. Honour him with your lips and life.

Glorify the LORD with me:

let us exalt his name together.

(Psalm 34:3)

Day 25

Read Ezekiel 40:1–16
Key verses: Ezekiel 40:1–2

....

> [1] *In the twenty-fifth year of our exile, at the beginning of the year, on the tenth of the month, in the fourteenth year after the fall of the city – on that very day the hand of the LORD was on me and he took me there.* [2] *In visions of God he took me to the land of Israel and set me on a very high mountain, on whose south side were some buildings that looked like a city.*

Have you ever been hill-walking? Sometimes it is not easy to see the path, and the climb is arduous. But when you reach the summit the view is spectacular.

From chapter 40 onwards Ezekiel takes us up a mountain and gives us a breathtaking view of an entirely new world, centred round the temple of God. Moses had gone up Mount Nebo and was allowed to see the Promised Land.

In this vision Ezekiel is also taken up a very high mountain and enabled to see the ultimate Promised Land, the new heavens and the new earth. Death Valley has now been raised above all the mountains of the world, and the temple of God is going to be established. Out of the resurrection life that God is going to breathe into people by his Word and Spirit, he is going to build a temple.

Notice the date in verse 1, 'In the twenty-fifth year of our exile, at the beginning of the year'. Ezekiel is mentioning this figure, twenty-five, because he is flagging up to those reading the book that they are half-way to the year of Jubilee (see also Ezekiel 46:17). Every fifty years, on the tenth day of the seventh month, the people of Israel celebrated a year of Jubilee. Slaves were released, the land was liberated from bondage, and debts were cancelled. The year of Jubilee becomes a great picture of salvation, the final vindication of God.

Ezekiel is prophesying to a people faced with the absence of God. He gives these exiles, with their temple destroyed and their city devastated, a glorious vision of what it will be like when God is present in all his fullness, might and power. He thrills their hearts with a vision of heaven and reminds them that they are almost there. They are on their way to the year of Jubilee, when they'll experience full salvation and the final vindication of God.

Take a trip up the mountain. Read God's description of heaven in Revelation 21 – 22. Soak up that spectacular view of God's new world and all he has planned for you. Today, if God seems silent, or if you face temptations, struggles and disappointments, hold on to that glorious vision. Hope in God and trust his promises.

Day 26

Read Ezekiel 43:1–12
Key verses: Ezekiel 43:1–5

....

¹ Then the man brought me to the gate facing east, ² and I saw the glory of the God of Israel coming from the east. His voice was like the roar of rushing waters, and the land was radiant with his glory. ³ The vision I saw was like the vision I had seen when he came to destroy the city and like the visions I had seen by the River Kebar, and I fell face down. ⁴ The glory of the LORD entered the temple through the gate facing east. ⁵ Then the Spirit lifted me up and brought me into the inner court, and the glory of the LORD filled the temple.

Ezekiel's vision is so graphic you can almost hear God's glory surging back into the temple.

In chapter 11 Ezekiel had seen a vision of the glory of the Lord departing from the Most Holy Place. Now in chapter 43 the description of the temple culminates in the glory of God coming back through the eastern door to be present with his people (verse 4).

The God who marched before Israel through the desert now lives with them on his holy hill. Of course, the Israelites never believed God's presence was tied to any geographical spot (2 Chronicles 6:18). While the temple represented the presence of God, it never limited it, for God was in the midst of his people. Ezekiel's ministry taught these exiles that the indestructible temple was the presence of God in glory among and with his people, wherever they found themselves (11:16).

Interestingly, Luke's Gospel begins in the temple with Jesus being brought in for dedication. Held in the hands of Simeon, he is described as 'the glory of your people Israel' (Luke 2:32), a title often used to refer to the temple. Where do we see the temple in the New Testament? Where is the radiance of God's glory? John says, 'We have seen his glory, the glory of the one and only Son, who came from the Father, full of grace and truth' (John 1:14).

John makes the link clearer when he records Jesus turning over the tables of the temple traders. Jesus wasn't simply making a statement against those who were ripping off the tourists coming to worship God. He halted the way the temple did its business; he suspended the process of offering sacrifices. And this led to a discussion about who Jesus was. The people asked for a sign. 'Jesus answered them, "Destroy this temple, and I will raise it again in three days." They replied, "It has taken forty-six years to build this temple, and you are going to raise it in three days?" But the temple he had spoken of was his body' (John 2:19–21).

You cannot read Ezekiel's description of that perfectly holy temple without using your New Testament to tell you that God's final perfect temple is Jesus.

The temple made without hands is the only authentic dwelling place for the glory of God. As the apostle Paul wrote, 'In Christ all the fullness of the Deity lives in bodily form' (Colossians 2:9).

Immanuel. God with us. Consider the magnitude of this. God is with you in hospital, during that difficult work meeting, as you speak to your child's head teacher, as you shop, as you talk with friends and as your home group meets together. Be encouraged and challenged that the very presence of Almighty God is with you wherever you go and whatever you do today.

Day 27

Read Ezekiel 43:10–27
Key verses: Ezekiel 43:10–12

....

> [10] *Son of man, describe the temple to the people of Israel, that they may be ashamed of their sins. Let them consider its perfection,* [11] *and if they are ashamed of all they have done, make known to them the design of the temple – its arrangement, its exits and entrances – its whole design and all its regulations and laws. Write these down before them so that they may be faithful to its design and follow all its regulations.*
> [12] *This is the law of the temple: all the surrounding area on top of the mountain will be most holy. Such is the law of the temple.*

Imagine the temple as a gate (see Ezekiel 48:30–35).

Like a gate, the temple provided access to God's presence. Many times a day people came to the temple to offer sacrifices, acknowledging they could only approach this holy God if their sins had been paid for.

At the same time the temple was also a gate keeping people out of God's presence. Gentiles couldn't get into the temple compound, women could get in only so far, men a bit further, priests further still, but only the high priest was able to get into the Most Holy Place, and that just once a year. The temple emphasized the barrier of sin that keeps people away from God.

So the temple is both a barrier and a means of access. It systematically excluded certain groups, kept others at a distance, but at the same time offered a way for people to come to know God.

The climax of Ezekiel's temple description is this massive altar which dominates the sanctuary. It is bigger than the altar described in Leviticus. It is bigger than the altar the Jews actually constructed when they rebuilt the temple. This altar signifies God's grace and welcome, and takes a central place because it is only by sacrifice that this reconciliation and acceptance take place.

But even the blood of goats and bulls couldn't take away sin (Hebrews 10:4). What sacrifice makes us absolutely acceptable to God? There is only one sacrifice for all time: the sacrifice of our Lord Jesus. He is the real gate (John 10:7–10).

> Therefore, brothers and sisters, since we have confidence to enter the Most Holy Place by the blood of Jesus, by a new and living way opened for us through the curtain, that is, his body, and since we have a great priest over the house of God, let us draw near to God with a sincere heart and with the full assurance that faith brings, having our hearts sprinkled to cleanse us from a guilty conscience and having our bodies washed with pure water.
> (Hebrews 10:19–22)

It is right to feel shame when we see our sin in the light of God's perfection (Ezekiel 43:10). Confess your sin, repent and turn to God for forgiveness (1 John 1:9). Christ's blood washes away your sin, so don't let Satan keep reminding you of your guilt. Memorize Hebrews 10:19–22; say it out loud; repeat these truths to yourself and let God's Word nourish your soul. Christ's death has completely dealt with your sin. God's wrath is satisfied. You are justified and forgiven. You are now 'in Christ'. Today, boldly enter God's presence and enjoy your restored relationship with your heavenly Father.

Day 28

Read Ezekiel 44:10–31

Key verses: Ezekiel 44:13, 15–16, 23

....

¹³ *They [the Levites who served idols] are not to come near to serve me as priests or come near any of my holy things or my most holy offerings; they must bear the shame of their detestable practices . . .*

¹⁵ *But the Levitical priests, who are descendants of Zadok and who guarded my sanctuary when the Israelites went astray from me, are to come near to minister before me; they are to stand before me to offer sacrifices of fat and blood, declares the Sovereign LORD.* ¹⁶ *They alone are to enter my sanctuary; they alone are to come near my table to minister before me and serve me as guards . . .*

²³ *They are to teach my people the difference between the holy and the common and show them how to distinguish between the unclean and the clean.*

What is happening inside the temple?

Ezekiel describes a reformed priesthood offering worship. It is a God-centred community, a holy people in a holy place.

Under the old covenant the people were separated from the priesthood. And we still tend to view holiness as something reserved for the spiritual elite – missionaries and ministers. But God's desire has always been that his people serve him as priests (Exodus 19). Christ's death has made that possible. As Peter explained, 'You are a chosen people, a royal priesthood, a holy nation, God's special possession, that you may declare the praises of him who called you out of darkness into his wonderful light' (1 Peter 2:9). We are that God-centred community, a holy people in a holy place, that Ezekiel spoke of.

So 'as you come to him, the living Stone – rejected by humans but chosen by God and precious to him – you also, like living stones, are being built into a spiritual house to be a holy priesthood, offering spiritual sacrifices acceptable to God through Jesus Christ' (1 Peter 2:4–5).

When we give generously to God's work, that is a fragrant offering, an acceptable sacrifice, pleasing to God. When we sing and celebrate what God has done, we are offering him a sacrifice of praise. And more than that, our whole lives can be offered as a living sacrifice to God (Romans 12:1).

These New Testament images of sacrifice and priesthood are taken straight out of Ezekiel and remind those of us who are Christians, indwelt by the Holy Spirit, that we are called to holiness.

It doesn't matter what label you might give yourself – you could be a student, a parent, unemployed or retired – your primary role is that of a priest. God has placed you in a specific context, with a specific set of relationships and responsibilities, to be his priest there. What does that look like for you? What are the spiritual sacrifices you are offering to God? How is your holiness making an impact? Ask for God's help to be his priest. Today, serve sacrificially, make every effort to be holy, and devote yourself to God and his work.

Day 29

Read Ezekiel 47:1–12
Key verses: Ezekiel 47:1, 12

....

[1] The man brought me back to the entrance to the temple, and I saw water coming out from under the threshold of the temple towards the east (for the temple faced east). The water was coming down from under the south side of the temple, south of the altar . . .

[12] [The stream became a river.] Fruit trees of all kinds will grow on both banks of the river. Their leaves will not wither, nor will their fruit fail. Every month they will bear fruit, because the water from the sanctuary flows to them. Their fruit will serve for food and their leaves for healing.

Whether you are in the Amazon jungle or the Highlands of Scotland, wherever a river flows there is life.

So notice that a river flows from the south side of the temple – interestingly, that's the place of sacrifice. Other prophets spoke of this. Joel prophesied of a day when a fountain would flow from the Lord's house (Joel 3:18). Zechariah said, 'On that day living water will flow out from Jerusalem' (Zechariah 14:8).

Jesus, the final temple, also used the image of a river bringing life. Sitting by the well with the Samaritan woman excluded from the temple he offered her a way to worship God. Jesus told her, 'Everyone who drinks this water will be thirsty again, but whoever drinks the water I give them will never thirst. Indeed, the water I give them will become in them a spring of water welling up to eternal life' (John 4:13–14).

Similarly in John 7:37–38: 'Jesus stood and said in a loud voice, "Let anyone who is thirsty come to me and drink. Whoever believes in me, as Scripture has said, rivers of living water will flow from within them." '

The river motif runs throughout Scripture, right to Revelation. In Revelation 22 the Lamb is among his people and God is there with them. We read that the river of the water of life, as clear as crystal, was flowing from the throne of God and from the Lamb. Ezekiel says that where that river flows, everything will live. It brings life and healing to the nations.

Jesus still offers living water. He said, 'I have come that they may have life, and have it to the full' (John 10:10).

Does your spiritual life feel stagnant? Perhaps you have tried many ways to jump-start it. But there is really only one way: come to Christ. Return to him and drink deeply: spend time in his presence, praying and reading his Word. Let his living waters cleanse you from sin, revive your soul and satisfy the deepest longings of your heart. We look forward to the day when God will renew the whole of creation, but you can experience renewal today. You can be a Psalm 1 Christian – refreshed and fruitful – if you plant your roots deep in Christ and drink from his life-giving stream.

Day 30

Read Ezekiel 48:1–35
Key verses: Ezekiel 48:29, 35

....

> [29] *'This is the land you are to allot as an inheritance to the tribes of Israel, and these will be their portions,' declares the Sovereign LORD . . .*
> [35] *'The distance all around will be 18,000 cubits.*
> *'And the name of the city from that time on will be:*
> THE LORD IS THERE.*

Are you spending your children's inheritance, or have your parents spent yours? Don't worry. Every child of God has a guaranteed inheritance!

In chapter 48 Ezekiel picks up the city metaphor again as he talks about the land that is the inheritance of God's people. Every tribe has a portion, an allotted space in this heaven Ezekiel is describing.

Remember the language Jesus uses in Matthew 5 when he quotes Psalm 37:11: 'The meek . . . will inherit the earth.' The word for 'earth' used here can be translated 'land'. Right now we don't have a land; we're still aliens and strangers. As the author of Hebrews explains, 'Here we do not have an enduring city, but we are looking for the city that is to come' (Hebrews 13:14). Ezekiel 48 is saying that in that city there will be a place for you.

Jesus likewise encouraged his disciples, 'My Father's house has many rooms; if that were not so, would I have told you that I am going there to prepare a place for you? And if I go and prepare a place for you, I will come back and take you to be with me that you also may be where I am' (John 14:2–3).

The book of Revelation picks up much of this imagery from Ezekiel's heavenly vision. John presents us with a new Jerusalem. In this new city the people of God are from both the old and the new covenants because the names of the apostles as well as the prophets are written on the foundations and walls of the city. All of God's people are there.

There is only one difference. John says, 'I did not see a temple in the city, because the Lord God Almighty and the Lamb are its temple' (Revelation 21:22). This is the definitive New Testament explanation of Ezekiel's vision. The Lord God Almighty and the Lamb are the city's temple. The entire city has become a holy place. There is no altar because the Lamb, the one who made the sacrifice, is at the heart of the new Jerusalem. Everyone who is there has got in because of the sacrifice he made on the cross.

Ezekiel's last words describe the city: 'THE LORD IS THERE.' And we hear the echo of John's words in Revelation 21:3: 'Look! God's dwelling-place is now among the people, and he will dwell with them. They will be his people, and God himself will be with them and be their God.'

Ezekiel's vision of heaven is our destiny. We are almost there.

What would make heaven heaven for you? An end to pain, seeing loved ones again, discovering the answers to all your questions? In truth, heaven will be heaven simply because God is there. Being with God and enjoying him for ever – this is your inheritance. While you wait, don't lose heart; don't let doubts or grief throw you off course. Stay faithful, keep pressing on: you are almost there!

For further study

If you would like to do further study on Ezekiel, the following books may be useful:

- Iain Duguid, *Ezekiel*, NIV Application Commentary (Zondervan, 1999).

- John Goldingay, *Lamentations and Ezekiel for Everyone* (SPCK, 2015).

- Derek Thomas, *God Strengthens: Ezekiel Simply Explained* (Evangelical Press, 2004).

- Christopher Wright, *The Message of Ezekiel*, The Bible Speaks Today (IVP, 2001).

KESWICK MINISTRIES

Our purpose

Keswick Ministries is committed to the spiritual renewal of God's people for his mission in the world.

God's purpose is to bring his blessing to all the nations of the world. That promise of blessing, which touches every aspect of human life, is ultimately fulfilled through the life, death, resurrection, ascension and future return of Christ. All of the people of God are called to participate in his missionary purposes, wherever he may place them. The central vision of Keswick Ministries is to see the people of God equipped, encouraged and refreshed to fulfil that calling, directed and guided by God's Word in the power of his Spirit, for the glory of his Son.

Our priorities

Keswick Ministries seeks to serve the local church through:

- *Hearing God's Word*: the Scriptures are the foundation for the church's life, growth and mission, and Keswick Ministries is committed to preaching and teaching God's Word in a way that is faithful to Scripture and relevant to Christians of all ages and backgrounds.

- *Becoming like God's Son*: from its earliest days the Keswick movement has encouraged Christians to live godly lives in the power of the Spirit, to grow in Christlikeness and to live under his lordship in every area of life. This is God's will for his people in every culture and generation.

- *Serving God's mission*: the authentic response to God's Word is obedience to his mission, and the inevitable result of Christlikeness is sacrificial service. Keswick Ministries seeks to encourage committed discipleship in family life, work and society, and energetic engagement in the cause of world mission.

Our ministry

- *Keswick: the event.* Every summer the town of Keswick hosts a three-week convention, which attracts some 15,000 Christians from the UK and around the world. The event provides Bible teaching for all ages, vibrant worship, a sense of unity across generations and denominations, and an inspirational call to serve Christ in the world. It caters for children of all ages and has a strong youth and young adult programme. And it all takes place in the beautiful Lake District – a perfect setting for rest, recreation and refreshment.

- *Keswick: the movement.* For 140 years the work of Keswick has had an impact on churches worldwide, and today the movement is underway throughout the UK, as well as in many parts of Europe, Asia, North America, Australia, Africa and the Caribbean. Keswick Ministries is committed to strengthening the network in the UK and beyond, through prayer, news, pioneering and cooperative activity.

- *Keswick resources.* Keswick Ministries produces a range of books and booklets based on the core foundations of Christian life and mission. It makes Bible teaching available through free access to mp3 downloads, and the sale of DVDs and CDs. It broadcasts online through Clayton TV and annual BBC Radio 4 services.

- *Keswick teaching and training.* In addition to the summer convention, Keswick Ministries is developing teaching and training events that will happen at other times of the year and in other places.

Our unity

The Keswick movement worldwide has adopted a key Pauline statement to describe its gospel inclusivity: 'for you are all one in Christ Jesus' (Galatians 3:28). Keswick Ministries works with evangelicals from a wide variety of church backgrounds, on the understanding that they share a commitment to the essential truths of the Christian faith as set out in its statement of belief.

Our contact details

T: 01768 780075
E: info@keswickministries.org
W: www.keswickministries.org
Mail: Keswick Ministries, Convention Centre, Skiddaw Street, Keswick CA12 4BY, England

Related titles from IVP

THE FOOD FOR THE JOURNEY SERIES

The Food for the Journey series offers daily devotionals from well-loved Bible teachers at the Keswick Convention in an ideal pocket-sized format – to accompany you wherever you go.

Available in the series

1 Thessalonians
Alec Motyer with Elizabeth McQuoid
978 1 78359 439 9

2 Timothy
Michael Baughen with Elizabeth McQuoid
978 1 78359 438 2

Ezekiel
Liam Goligher with Elizabeth McQuoid
978 1 78359 603 4

Hebrews
Charles Price with Elizabeth McQuoid
978 1 78359 611 9

James
Stuart Briscoe with Elizabeth McQuoid
978 1 78359 523 5

John 14 – 17
Simon Manchester with Elizabeth McQuoid
978 1 78359 495 5

Ruth
Alistair Begg with Elizabeth McQuoid
978 1 78359 525 9

Praise for the series

'This devotional series is biblically rich, theologically deep and full of wisdom . . . I recommend it highly.' Becky Manley Pippert, speaker, author of *Out of the Saltshaker and into the World* and creator of the Live/Grow/Know course and series of books

'These devotional guides are excellent tools.' John Risbridger, Chair of Keswick Ministries, and Minister and Team Leader, Above Bar Church, Southampton

'These bite-sized banquets . . . reveal our loving Father weaving the loose and messy ends of our everyday lives into his beautiful, eternal purposes in Christ.' Derek Burnside, Principal, Capernwray Bible School

'I would highly recommend this series of 30-day devotional books to anyone seeking a tool that will help [him or her] to gain a greater love of scripture, or just simply . . . to do something out of devotion. Whatever your motivation, these little books are a must-read.' Claud Jackson, *Youthwork* Magazine

Available from your local Christian bookshop or **www.ivpbooks.com**

Related teaching CD packs

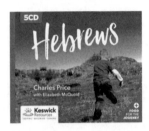

Ezekiel
Liam Goligher
SWP2263D (5-CD pack)
SWP2263A (5-DVD pack)

Hebrews
Charles Price
SWP2281D (5-CD pack)

ALSO AVAILABLE

SWP2203D
(5-CD pack)

SWP2202D
(4-CD pack)

SWP2239D
(4-CD pack)

SWP2238D
(5-CD pack)

SWP2238A
(5-DVD pack)

SWP2280D
(5-CD pack)

SWP2280A
(5-DVD pack)